Library of Congress Control Number: 2019906392
ISBN: Softcover   978-1-7960-3659-6
        Hardcover   978-1-7960-3660-2
        EBook   978-1-7960-3658-9

Print information available on the last page

Rev. date: 07/15/2019

To order additional copies of this book, contact:
Xlibris
1-888-795-4274
www.Xlibris.com
Orders@Xlibris.com

Ninnie's
Alphabet Rhyming
Babies

Dedication

This book is dedicated to all of my children that I had the wonderful opportunity of keeping in my Day Care throughout the years. I am so thankful that they are a part of my life!

Proverbs #22: 6
Train up a child in the way that he should go: and when he is old, he will not depart from it.

Mark #10: 14

Suffer the little children to come unto me, and forbid them not: for of such is the kingdom of God.

A is for...

Alligator

Apple

Adalyn

Analeigh

Alexa

Adyn

Ant

Avery

Abby

Ansley

Alana

A's A's
Everywhere!
Playing here,
playing there.
Swinging from
vines and jumping
ropes, hula-hoops,
sand and scoops.

1

B is for...

Bear

Brantleigh

Briley P.

Briley L.

Bryce

Bentley

Braeden

Brax

Brendan

Braydon

Barrett

B's B's
Bats, balls, and bounce,
if you please.
Drawing a house and a yellow
sun, we are having so much fun!

Butterfly

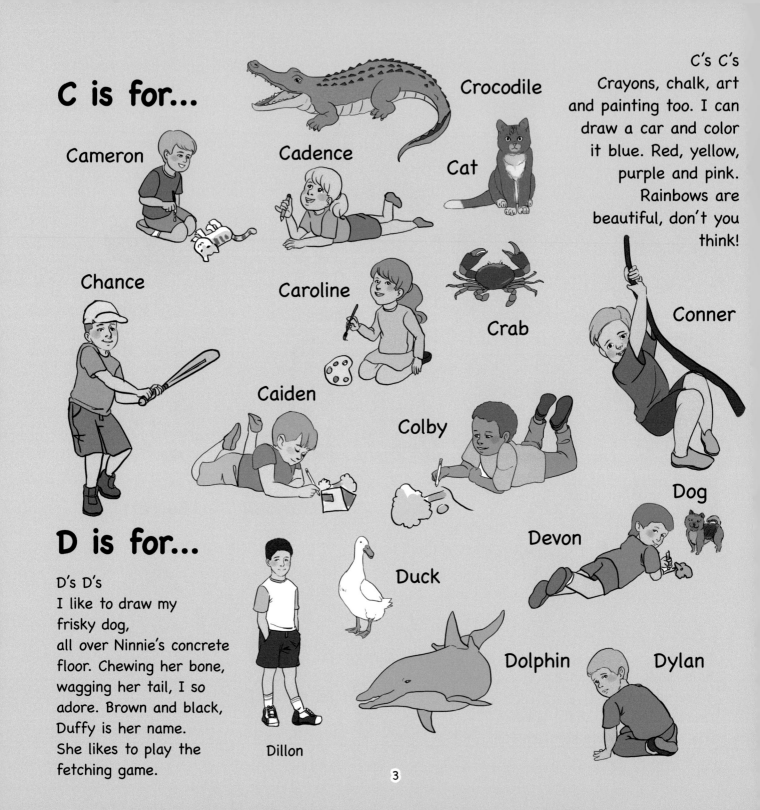

C is for...

Crocodile

Cameron

Cadence

Cat

C's C's
Crayons, chalk, art and painting too. I can draw a car and color it blue. Red, yellow, purple and pink. Rainbows are beautiful, don't you think!

Chance

Caroline

Crab

Conner

Caiden

Colby

Dog

D is for...

Devon

Duck

D's D's
I like to draw my frisky dog,
all over Ninnie's concrete floor. Chewing her bone, wagging her tail, I so adore. Brown and black, Duffy is her name. She likes to play the fetching game.

Dolphin

Dylan

Dillon

E is for...

Elephant

Ethan

Emerson

E's E's
Jumping, skipping, hopping and flipping. Be real careful that you don't fall down. That would hurt to hit your crown. Running and bouncing a basketball, shooting the hoops and feeling tall. E is also for elephant, huge with a long trunk. When scared by a mouse, will show a lot of spunk.

Fox

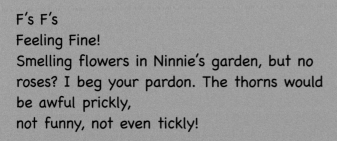

F is for...

Flowers

F's F's
Feeling Fine!
Smelling flowers in Ninnie's garden, but no roses? I beg your pardon. The thorns would be awful prickly,
not funny, not even tickly!

G is for...

Gavin

Gianna

Giraffe

Gunner

Griffen

Green Butterfly

Golden Dandelions

Grasshopper

G's G's
Golly Gee Golly!
Watching a green grasshopper jump high, I feel like he could touch the sky.
Look at the dandelions blowing in the breeze, they touched my nose and made me sneeze.
One blew up to a green butterfly and landed on top.
They fluttered away and didn't stop.

5

H is for...

Hippo

Hunter K.

Hannah
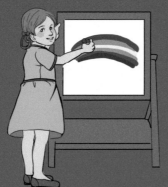

H's H's
Outside we go to our playhouse, a
warm and cozy place,
with pretty curtains in the
window,all made from lace.
Drawing squares on the ground,
with numbers from 1-10.
Hopscotch is the game that we
play, and I bet that I can win!
Throwing the pebble,then jump
single-double,
all the way to square numbered
10, without any trouble.

House
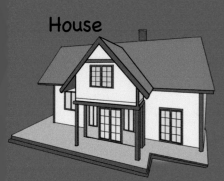

Harper

Hunter A.
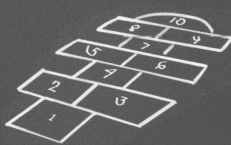

I is for...

Ice Cream

I's I's
Three scoops of ice cream
with vanilla, strawberry,
chocolate and sprinkles, such a fun day.
Add bananas on the side and you have
an ice cream sundae. Sticky on my
fingers and oh so good to me, skipping
along and happy as I can be.

Iguana

Hopscotch

J is for...

Jayden

Jellyfish

Jelly Beans

Jaedon

Jada

Jagger

Jake

Jacks

Joseph "Joe"

J's J's
Throwing Jacks and playing Jigsaw Alphabet.
Chutes and Ladders, Candyland, Checkers and Old Maid, don't
forget Monopoly, because you get paid.
Googly eyes and Dominoes, fun in the pool with the water hose.

K is for...

Kite

Kaylan

Kellie

Kangaroo

Kensley

Kody

K's K's
Flying up so high is my colorful kite, taking off in majestic flight. Way up in the sky, blowing left and blowing right. It seems to touch the clouds in a way, breezing around on this sunny day.

L is for...

Lacey

Lane

Laegen

Langston

Lion

Lacey

Ladybug

Leaf

L's L's
Watching the ladybugs in the grass so small, red with black spots. They landed on a flower, during an April shower. Summer goes by and we go on a nature walk, finding acorns and rocks that are round. Leaves blowing in the air during Autumn. Red, yellow, orange and brown.

M is for...

Monkey

Maddie

Madison

Mason

Max

M's M's
Swinging around
like a monkey
you see, eating
our snacks like a
chimpanzee. Playing
red rover as a
team is fun,
sending your friend
to break the link,
when you run. Fast
as I can to get
through this race,
I like the
excitement at a
fast pace.

Maggie

Michael

Matthew

Morgan L.

Moose

Morgan H.

McKenzie

9

N is for...

Narwhal

Noah

Nora

Ninnie

N's N's
Ninnie loves us very much,
baking us cookies with her
loving touch. She has worked
hard through the years.
Keeping us clean, nourished,
fed and always wiping away
our tears.
Joy always comes from above,
God helps us with his love.

Natalie

Oval

O is for..

Owl

Octopus

O's O's
Oval shapes and round shapes,
squares, rectangles, and triangle
shapes. We can imagine all sorts
of things
that these shapes can be.
We can put a circle and triangle
together and make a tree.

P is for...

Panda

Porcupine

Parker H.

Parker B.

Purple rocks

Purple cars, trucks, dumpers, and bulldozers

P's P's
Purple cars, trucks, dumpers and bulldozers, scraping paths and digging in the mud, dropping it down with a big thud.
Piling up rocks to make a mountain. Splashing the water from the fountain.

Q is for...

Quail

Quiet

Q's Q's
Quiet as a mouse at
naptime, Ninnie reads us
a book.
Adventures on an Island with Chip-A-Hoy and
Captain Hook.
We close our eyes and dream of a wonderful place,
with coconut, mango and kiwi trees blowing all
around.
We hear bongo drums on this Island making a
beating sound.

Rocket

Rowen

Rabbit

R is for...

Racoon

R's R's
Riding the bicycle down the hill.
We will have fun, I bet you a
dollar bill. Twirling and whirling
around we go, when will we stop,
no one will know.
Can't stop now, we are having too
much fun.
Sweat pouring down in the
bright sun.

S is for...

Seahorse

Seal

Starfish

Snake

Squirrel

Space

Sawyer

Seager

Skyler

S's S's
We think about what could be in outer space, the moon, stars, comets fly by without a trace. Could there be another world, out in the galaxy?
Are there aliens, creatures with antennas on their head? Who knows, maybe?

T is for...

Tiger

Tahj

Tree

Turtle

Taylor

Unicorn

Umbrella

T's T's
Tippy toes, playing hide
and seek.
Count from 1-20 and
don't you peek.
Round the corner, here
I come.
Blowing a big piece of
bubble gum.

U is for...

U's U's
Unicorns are my favorite
horse,
with a pointed horn on the
top of their head.
I could ride one up to a
rainbow, with no dread. I
wouldn't be scared, not at all,
because my unicorn friend
would not let me fall.
Up and over that rainbow
bright,
to the stars that shine like a
night light.

V is for...

V's V's
We pretend to take a
voyage, out across the
mighty sea. Flowing,
fluttering like a goose, we
pretend to be.
Just then I saw geese flying
south for the winter,
in the shape of a V.
Made a loud honking sound
and startled me.

Vampire bat

Voyage

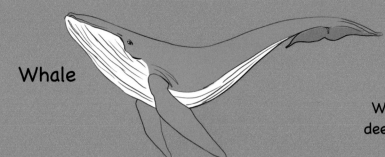
Whale

W is for...

W's W's
Watching a whale, swimming deep in the ocean. He flipped up high out of the water, in slow motion. Playing in the water with this wild imagination, at the sand and water table. Creating so many stories, from so many fables. Whistling my favorite song. I could stay on the playground, all day long.

Will B.

Will S.

Willam

Worm

Watermelon

X-Ray fish

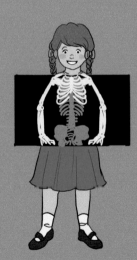
x-Ray girl

X is for...

X's X's
When I look at an x-ray,
I can see all of my bones. Long, short, big and small, they will grow and I will be tall. Growing like a flower in a meadow, as far as I can see.
Sunshine beams down on them, pretty as can be!

Y is for...

Yak

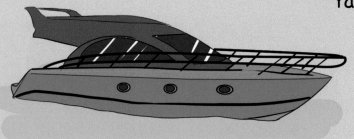

Yacht

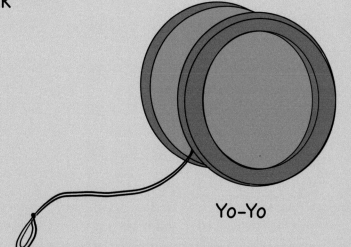

Yo-Yo

Z is for...

Zebra

Zoo

Zipper

Zig-Zag

I was born Jacqueline Michelle Price, in the small town of Alma, Georgia. I grew up on a farm with wonderful parents and grandparents. I learned Christian values and was loved very much. I am married to William Christopher McQuaig and I live in Douglas, Georgia. My parents are Jack and Barbara Price of Alma, Georgia. I have one sister. I have two sons, one daughter and eight grandchildren. Enjoying a wonderful Day Care in my home, keeping children for 17 years. I am very thankful for the love of my children and their parents and I love them very much.

I also wrote three other books that I think you will enjoy with your family!

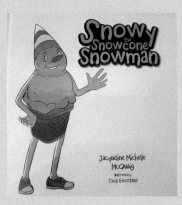

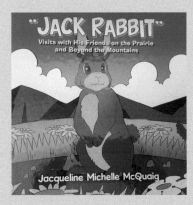

Printed in the United States
By Bookmasters